THE KNOWLEDGE

The Knowledge
Robert Peake

ISBN: 978-0-9931201-1-4

First published April 2015 by:

Nine Arches Press
PO Box 6269
Rugby
CV21 9NL
United Kingdom
www.ninearchespress.com

Printed in Britain by:

The Russell Press Ltd.

THE KNOWLEDGE

Robert Peake

Nine
Arches
Press

for Valerie

Contents

The Smoke

"The penalty for education is self-consciousness. But it is too late for ignorance."

– Marvin Bell, '32 Statements About Poetry'

The Argument

White Pigeons

are not doves. They do not stand
for peace, but flock and swoop
above my head in the blue before dawn.

They are a liquid in the air,
elastic, bunching and swarming
like oil drops on water.

I do not want to know the physics.
I do not want to make a documentary.
I stand and watch them ripple like a flag.

The soldier inside me wants to salute.
The prophet takes it for a sign.
They double-back, like a bed sheet, folded.

And then they dip below the tree line,
leaving their absence to hang in the air.
I never wished they were more than they were.

A mourning dove now sounds his call to prayer.
A red-tailed hawk lords over mousing fields.
I have heard some call all pigeons *wingèd rats*.

But these were different, bred to home,
which means that they were practising,
and work never seemed as elegant as this.

Tie a message to my foot. I will assume
my place in the aerial formation. Let me
be a single snowflake in that flurry.

Still Life with Bougainvillea

The bougainvillea taps
at the window, and you

are gone. The cat watches
over the path where you

might return. I watch
the cat, and the small

flowers inside the flowers,
as they brush the pane.

On the cat, there are fleas.
In the flowers, flowers.

In me, your absence drums its
fingers at the points

where I notice my pulse, taps
its beak against the bars

of my chest. Small creature
in my own creature body,

white flowers enveloped in red.

Amuse-Bouche

A dollop of cream from your own
mother's milk, seasoned with tears
from the first girl you kissed,
garnished with coarse-cut parsley,
served in a snail's shell.

Lint from your best-loved jumper
sprinkled with grains of a childhood sandbox,
wax shavings from your preschool crayons
nettles from the banks of the pollywog pond
all arranged in a favourite lunch pail.

Of course, for dessert, we have madeleines,
to dip in a tea made of vapour and dust,
sweet-smelling, like the home of your elderly aunt,
which dissolve upon contact and waking. Go on.
Have another. You will never be full.

The Argument

The bees make a mask, rippling like sauce,
covering the beekeeper's eyelids. He shaves
them off with a credit card, the stench
of pollen clotting his nostrils, the logic
of terror unable to win its case, though
tiny legs tap their reasons across his pores.
The argument to remain placid is as soft
as the fur-covered thoraces, as clear
and as light as the transparent wings.
Do nothing. Breathe through your teeth.
In swarm, a cloud of electric current,
but here, on the contours of his face,
they seem to wander tip-toe, sleepy,
navigating over each other with compound
vision, kaleidoscopic-sighted pilgrims
oblivious to one another on their quest,
brushing the tips of their long fore-wings
against the keeper's eyelashes,
as close to kissing as they will come,
bound together without intimacy,
curling under each other like a slow-
motion rioting mob, a water ballet
where the music is stillness, is tapping,
the brush of abdomen, antennae, and legs.

Robin

Bold and tattered, slashing into view,
tiny courtier teeming with invidious mites,

we welcome you at the waterspout, bent sprig,
weaving a maypole out of long oat grass.

You wear a red-crossed breast, poor Templar,
far from healthy with your half-feathered head,

blandishing the cold-snapped air, informing
and interpreting the seasons like a wild-eyed monk.

You preach through the frost and meandering drizzle,
moot points of theology and tactics with squirrels,

piecemeal captain of our sinking green ship,
perched like Nelson at the tallest crow's nest.

Guide us, our skipper, bard and troubadour, into
the winter you know will be your last.

Grass-Talkers

I am the grass. I will not tell you
how to live. However, in addition

to ground cover, and grave cover,
I can offer the following services:

an emetic for overfull dogs and cats,
something to water when the orchids all die,

and a better place to fall than concrete.
Think of photosynthesis as your friend.

Do not ask me to symbolize the ones
you love. I will not whisper *be patient*

or *endure*. What I say is audible
only to ants and wood lice.

Do not ask *What next?* unless
you are ready for the answer.

And do not ask anything of me. Unless
you want to roll yourself downhill.

The clover can tell who is going to die.
I know who the wind loves best, however,

you mustn't say you heard this from me.
Such people they remove from mainstream life.

The Flies

Why the long face? I'll tell you.
The maggots in my shit become flies.
The flies seek out my weeping eyes.
They cluster in silver-black tears.

I have scavenged the field to its stubs.
The dust whips my face, drawing tears.
The flies excavate my nostrils and ears
seeking sweat, saliva, and blood.

I toss my head for a moment's relief,
fling them off like droplets of tar,
they spray, congeal, return to scar
my face with switchblade wings.

Why the long face? You tell me.
Do you cry out for a breath of wind
to blow the flies from your skin,
carrying the scent of your mother?

I have scoured the field for her smell
while the flies pore over my face
knitting a veil of silver-black lace
to cover my eyes from the day.

Badger

Here come the dog-toothed questions,
with nothing behind you but wall.

Ursula

Black hair. Red claws. That's all
you need to know. She left
the cubs a long time ago,
and now all she wants is a man
to drink gin and play snooker.
She keeps a gun in her purse
and two ex-lovers in jail,
signs her letters with a kiss
and a dab of cheap perfume.
She knows how to use a letter opener,
walk upright like a lady,
forage berries in the forest,
bandage a gunshot wound,
claw her way out of the trunk
of a speeding car, and roll away.
She's on the hunt when hunted,
growls obscenities when hit
by a tranquilizer dart.
In this city full of garbage,
she knows you by your smell.

The Hills

It is
too late
in the year
for such weeping,
I tell you, be still,
the winds of our sighing
have left the hills in disarray
and it is late, now, for us
to be singing like this,
undressed, together,
speaking quietly,
as if to forget
just how late.
It is just.
How late?
As if to forget
speaking quietly,
undressed together,
to be sighing like this.
And it is late, now, for us,
to have left the hills in disarray,
the winds of our singing.
I tell you, be still
for such weeping.
In the year
too late.
It is.

"I Was Born to Small Fish."

– from a mistranslated line by Pablo Neruda

They fill the stream with dashes,
clot in dark collections by the bank,
a clutch of minnows sprayed
into life, like torpedoes
from a pregnant submarine.

And I am born unto them,
child of the sardine, goldfish,
pollywog—whatever can swim
in a thimble, dodge change
flipped into a fountain
for luck.

      I am not the son
of the marlin, the sturgeon—
the sunfish, around whom
jellyfish revolve like planets.
The smallest of fish
is sufficient to be my mother.

I am from this line of stream-
swimmers, gulf-swimmers, fish
at the mercy of eddies
and wakes, schooling together,
and bursting apart, confusion
and numbers our only defence,
this line, this arc—

                  hundreds flashing
through a shaft of light—
I call them *family* and
comrades, call them
my fish, small fish, birthright.

Adelphophagy

"The ingestion by a developing larva of other eggs
or larvae from the same brood." —*OED*

I.

Brother-eater, you are the one
who survived the jailhouse womb

by devouring the other inmates.
Two nurse shark will emerge

from a conceived brood of dozens,
kept apart in separate chambers,

feeding on their younger kin,
once free, the eldest lies in wait.

My colleague tells the story
of taping her younger sister

into a cardboard box, then denying
any knowledge of where she was.

Do sharks know that to be eaten
is terrifying and painful?

Or are they simply doing
what delights the teeth and jaw,

what pleases the throat in passing,
and cools the stomach's furnace?

II.

Brother-eater, you survived.
This much we can say for sure.

I do not recall what you sound like
after twenty-five years apart, only

you being older, I wanted to do whatever
you did, eat your food, mimic your walk.

Half-brother, I am part-ways you,
mirror held at an angle, consumer

of similar resources: language, music,
film, art, estrangement, speckled hope.

But I was the one our father raised,
printing my flesh with his fins,

while a stepfather taught you to swim
through the kelp-dark waters.

Nocturne with Writer's Block

Five days, and no letters sent to my other self.
It has been too long I have listened to chatter.
Now, let the deeper words come.

My poems protest the way I have lived my life.
Little poems, don't do that. I have lived
like anyone else, halfway entranced.

Nothing I can say will console them now.
All day, as I peer into a lighted screen,
leaves flash green and gold behind my eyes.

At night, while the TV flickers and babbles,
wind plays in the trees, high up and far away.
Let this poem speak back to them.

Let this poem speak to the birds, also,
nesting in those trees behind my eyes,
defying the garbage trucks and leaf blowers

with their songs praising potassium in the soil,
passing through the puce bodies of earthworms,
as they telescope through darkness in the clay.

Now it is getting late, and still the inside world
refuses to come out. The birds will settle for seeds
on the ground, and I will fall asleep to talk shows.

In my dreams, I am both wind and tree, the sound
and the feel of it. Each leaf I am is turning,
my only goal to catch the sun, to catch the sun.

Perhaps, like the leaf, this poem will never end,
but go on casting back the light until it fades.
Perhaps I have held it hostage long enough,

turning on its thin, cylindrical stalk. Forgive me,
this nostalgia for my own invented world.
Sometimes the one I live in seems unbearable.

Sometimes the light behind my eyes
becomes more real, and dazzling, because
I want it to be real, even as I am not.

For five days, I have been nothing but real.
Time to shed that skin, and write.
Time to spin, like a child, into blindness.

Here are the muted utterings of the night—
those monks, the crickets, are building a
rhythm, spinning their prayer-wheel legs.

In the distance, a piano is being played
by someone who also enjoys the cover of night.
Five days of stillness, and a night of spinning—

what next? The green and gold of a blessèd life.
Let the stillness come again, now I am ready.
Let the darkness take me down into the well.

British Matches

On the matchbox, there is a child,
frown like a downturned slice of melon
flames decorating her thin stick arms.

A single red wing arcs in salute
by the epigram: *Fire Kills Children.*
Above it is the royal coat of arms.

I wonder why only children. Fire kills
trees, and adults, too—anything alive,
once enfolded in that wing will soon

hear the *shhh* of death's librarian.
My father taught me games with matches.
We used to make rockets by wrapping

the match head in foil, propping it
on a bent paperclip, then tickling
the shiny underside with a flame.

It would fizz into the air, dangling
smoke like a dancer's scarf. I went
through whole booklets that way.

Now we are six thousand miles apart,
and the pale light of an unfamiliar
place lights up this new-to-me warning.

In the absence of photojournalism,
the idea of a child on fire
is as cartoonish as a queen

whose family symbols are national
symbols, propped up by a unicorn
in a place that will never be home.

Matins With Slippers And House Cat

Gumshoe is the sound of no sound.
The squeak of a dress shoe on linoleum rings
distinct from a sneaker on a hardwood court.
The sneak of the squeak is what matters.
I sit here in a squeaky chair, trying not to.
I position myself for zero-gravity effect.
Whole nations are attempting the same:
how to occupy the space between squeak
and no-squeak, that is the question.

My feet find their way into worn slippers.
The toes know to curl up for grip.
I pad through the house, in search of a snack,
some tea, or a book of poems. I glide.
The cat comes in to my office to question me.
She wants to know where I have hidden the dry food.
She wails as though she were starving, or mad.
I tell her that, after the French revolution, churches
were used to store grain. I spin in my chair for effect.

She is unimpressed. She only wants to know if
such an act would have brought mice to the altar.
I argue against utilitarianism. She leaves.
I have seen the sweat of nations bead on the brow
of the common worker. I have pilfered the ash cans
of Democracy, looking for butts. I have told
the priest his collar is guillotine-proof.
I have seen them in the night, rubbing chicken
blood on the rough wounds of the statues.

"Have A Nice Day!"

Have, why not?, instead, a day
of kumquats, instead
hold butter in your mouth
until the daymelt
and the dewy pulse
of reason hurdles slipwise
through the air.

Have a calendar of honeycomb,
fingers pricked
by daylight's sneeze.
Have at it! Have whatever
drainpipe song
the rush and surge
of garden leaves can sing.

Have a day bedecked in drops
of kerosene, and nights
lit only by reflecting snow.
Have a wedding. Have a funeral.
Get top marks
on a Rorschach test
from a greasy paper bag.

I wish you this: a hairpin day,
rivers re-liquidized in daylight,
the top rolled down on everything,

and streamers of the vaporous dark
scattered like tyrants
and cockroaches
under a lit, swinging bulb.

Have the cure within your reach,
and choose, instead, tap water.
Make milk from the milkweed,
and an occasion of the mundane,
when applauding a chorus
of baritone frogs,
wear the unnecessary tie.

Have a handstand day, a head-
stand day. Stand upon your limpid heart.
Have a moose day. The kind with horns.
Have a noose day, where the slipknot
slips, a getaway, a fast car
and jump in to it, stuffing fistfuls
of cash on the breeze.

Have it your way, kiddo,
and have it with jam.
Have sticky fingers for the neighbour's
roses, and pollen on your forehead
instead of ash. Have bees in every
bonnet, turn every phrase
impolite. Have any day. Pick one.

April

Barmaids pull green spiral taps,
tippling the bees in swarm
frothing up a golden head of pollen.

O the youthfulness of arrogance.
Blackbirds swap their arcane ciphers,
hacking into the un-redacted news.

Squirrels in fiasco groove the bark
to a barber-pole double helix,
shift a confetti of godsend petals.

Here is the sallow-green heart of things,
sap coursing through like amphetamine,
the sticky truth, its plausible deniability.

The soil steams with overfed grubs,
a richness of embarrassment—on goes
the arms race towards the beating sun.

Sometimes I Wonder What I Do

The hand that snaps the twig
from the branch is my hand, not tending
or pruning, but pausing
while walking to grab, and grasp,
and strain the bough thought-
lessly as I pass. I regard
the minor damage undaunted,
some juniper berries shook free
and crushed to a fibrous pulp,
and I do not demur to question
why my curling hand would hoard
up leaves, if it could, all along
the short path home — grabbing
sticks to smack the fence posts'
slats and picking the tight buds
of neighbours' roses, unrepentant,
my five fingers the whole city council,
judge, jury, and executioner,
and my thumb elected mayor, nay
governor, nay monarch, of the wax-leaf
picturesqueness, the possessive
pride and hard-pew reverence
of well-kept suburbs, sleepy
hamlets — the cow that knows
that grass belongs in the chambers
of her stomach, the goat that nibbles
tweed and rush and tarpaulin,
the gentle, absentminded anarchy

of plucking at the neighbourhood
like fur for fleas, like cotton
for seeds, picking, and picking
the whole damn place apart.

Postcards from the War Hospital

Last Gasp

December 30th, 2006

The scorpion is an opportunist for sure.
For days he waits in a desert hole,
the heat driving his prey toward the shade.

Once, a deposed tyrant hid in a hole,
breathing dust and ash, unable to stand.
When we found him, we hanged him.

The lungs balloon and drain
eighteen thousand times per day.
One day the alveoli all flash shut together.

One man's last breath is Baghdad city air.
Another drowns on his feet in chlorine gas.
Desdemona breathed the perfume of her bedclothes.

There are mothball-scented chambers in a life,
dark places moonlight cannot light up blue—
a held breath that the breather knows is final.

Dare we mention the soft grasses
growing, somehow, underneath a stone?
They, too, must have known the sunlight once.

A salt stain bleaches the pillow cover.
Who can tell if it was tears, saliva, or sweat?
Only that the head was wanting rest,

only that the fluids of the human animal
cannot be contained in sleep, in love, in death.
Some call the incognito *intimate*.

The chambers of our secrecy are vast.
While sleeping in his hole, our tyrant dreamt
of the high, gilded ceilings of his ballrooms.

More intricate than Arabesque tile,
the workings of a mind in flight, glimmering
and expansive as a polished marble floor.

Postcards from the War Hospital, Autumn

The leaves are silvering
in a patch of sun,
the grey leaves, catching light.
The sister of Patience
is Suffering. Grey wool skirts,
a nurse's cap. The end of ends.

Nothing more prismatic than
a pirate film at the matinee:
dust in a shaft of light.

The leaves are sleeping
in a patch of darkness.
Let them. They have earned it.

Cold morning. Cold night.
In between: the radiator
groans like a sore old man.

The leaves are decomposing.
Unseen creatures eat away.
The gangrene has come back.

Despot's Progress

I dictate in all weathers, including the warm ones,
at a cock-eyed angle, at a balmy degree, with latitude
stretching like a sock across toes; I am writing
a new first-person historic account of my greatness.

Do not frown, my downcast daffodil, we will educate
the appalling masses out of their brawn and head-banging,
forcing the miners to march in light, mincing steps
and eat the thinnest pancakes dusted in icing sugar.

We will drag them into the buoyant train stations
of tomorrow, letter by letter and note by note,
coercing the birds to sing from our national songbook
and shit on the fallen statues of lesser men.

Only the most beautiful women from the most beautiful
villages will be allowed near my coffin to mourn, to shed
tears on demand with an approved mineral content, pageant
veterans turning the good side of their anguish to camera.

Unidentified Photo on the Internet

The seaweed men patrol the icy town
with sticks wrapped in bumbergrass
their hooked beaks hissing steam,
eyes painted white against the dawn.

They trudge the streets like shaggy
marionettes, boots cracking glazed tarmac,
past tiny houses asleep in banks of snow.
The white mountain looks down on suburbia.

Bracken-clad and thistle-shod, the watchmen
pause, two fuzzy pillars holding up the sky.
Who are these fur-girded sentinels, guarding
the precarious stillness, listening for a shot?

Legume-coloured pantaloons, be proud.
I couldn't find your names on Wikipedia.
If you shed tears from those golf-ball eyes,
I'll be none the wiser, and very far away.

The green men mock us with their small parade,
marching in line, then two abreast, bumber-
sticks perched on their left shoulders,
palace guards unblinking in time of jubilee.

Everything has a name, a place, a purpose.
But when two green life-size puppets appear
in an elderly neighbour's hedgerow, do you
ask them in for tea, or hide the china?

Mr Ergosum Speaks

(after Zbigniew Herbert)

None of it matters. Let me say
that again: once, it mattered, and now,
when I snap my fingers, only dust.

That absurd cake! Justice. How it tilts
in layers on its pedestal, while party-goers
observe, *How remarkably straight.*

My hat is a chimney, chugging with promise.
What I think becomes soft smoke in the dampened air.
My coat-tails wave a continual flurry of goodbyes.

The nineteenth century was my favourite. Yes,
I have seen them all, through my monocle—
the one present I kept from the deposed Tsar.

All of it matters, actually, to the ants
on the sidewalk, hustling their minuscule lives.
Who can tell if they are small or just far away?

I wipe a tear from the corner of my eye.
The air, full of soot, encourages such weeping.
I wear a monogrammed kerchief in place of a heart.

Problem

It's not a problem problem. It's just a problem for the person whose problems are more important than yours, or anyone's. So now it is your problem, please drop everything, including your trousers, our customary salute. The problem will not go away by itself, though intervention may compound it, in which case you become the problem, and must, I'm afraid, be shot. Please treat this as a matter of some urgency. Problems like this don't come around every day. Please hold out your hand for the branding iron. Please hold out your hand for the paycheque. Please don't tell anyone about our-little-secret problem, please be sure to finish up half an hour ago. Problems like this are a daily occurrence. You must learn to prioritise, must learn to write your name clearly at the bottom of every invisible list. Please submit the solution in mirror writing. Please submit in all nine official languages. Please submit to the problem, please admit publicly that the problem has always been you.

Blessing the Bankers

"no raindrop / feels responsible / for the flood"
— despair.com, 2009

They are still out there, the stars, commanding
more depth than ever. The light from Venus

seems closer than is safe, more luminous
than a bad idea ablaze in an innocent mind.

But what is innocent? We think, at first, a baby,
upon whose face the weather moves in bursts,

who has not discovered volume control
and empties his bellowed lungs with wailing.

Here, too, in the dusk of life, we wail.
We thought the good times would never end,

forgot the dams were built against bursting,
how terrible the water, still and black.

We troubled no-one with our dreaming.
The surface of the sky went on with changes.

The blessings laid by our mothers on our foreheads—
let this one live a simple life, uncomplicated—

catch fire beneath the weak-but-omnipresent moon.
Let this one be a banker, made of bricks.

Even the tear-down crews are out of work, must find
something else to pull against, at home.

It is winter still, though it feels like spring.
The newspapers print ads for filing bankruptcy—

such a word, the rupture of banking, piling up,
as along the edge of a river—banks

to guard against the overspill, the rebel wave,
the slow rising water, seeking the floodplain.

Gather that child into your arms, the one you
hoped was owed a simple life. The waters rise.

The Rouchomovsky Skeleton

c. 1896, sold at Sotheby's in 2013 for $365,000

Perched on the edge of his velvet-lined coffin,
this tiny human skeleton in gold is ready
to buy us all a round of drinks, swinging
his jaw open in an all-too easy smile.
Then laid to rest, the jaw is set, hand-
bones crossed where his heart would be,
as if clutching a bouquet of flowers,
determination filling his sockets.

What does it say about vanity to replicate
our own human bones in golden filigree?
A Roman general once forced his slave to march
behind him in his triumphant hour, whispering
above the roar of the crowd: *You will die.*
Unparalleled, irreplaceable, this little status
symbol reminds us that our status also dies.
Now who is laughing? The heirloom lives on.

Petite *memento mori*, minuscule *vanitas*,
we cover you with a lid depicting Death
shouldering his scythe, leading a harvest
of souls into a mist-choked Netherworld—
or is it smoke and fire? An ocean wave?
The ground is littered with skulls,
the border alternates roses and thorns,
infants laughing and crying, both grotesque.

The headboard depicts a lyre, paintbrush, book,
and above it a baby gargoyle laughs in delight
at the delicate craft of the bare human hand.
The footing is the shield, helmet, and halberd,
and here a tiny thorn-wracked face contorts,
reflecting the art of war, carefully wrought
in precious metal, gurning back the consequence
when that same hand takes the gauntlet.

He strikes his poses effortlessly, this priceless
man-made skeleton-in-the-box. But was the slave
pouring humility into the general's ear? Or was
his reminder to make the moment somehow sweeter,
more precious for its transience, the echoing cheers—
the perfect pure-gold ribs, kneecaps, and teeth—
the chance to spend a lifetime's earnings beating
death for once by taking it all up, carefully, in hand?

Soldier at the Tomb of Alexander

They are laying the coins on your eyes,
for passage across the river, into death.

Your hands could never hold an olive branch,
zombie-like expression, face a pale shade.

So this is your overthrow, unable to
side-step mortality, and a sarcophagus

will be your war tent, heaped with
your belongings, raised up from the soil.

What good will they do for you now?
Better to bury a snowball in the ground,

or the nutty scent of almonds, a particle
of sand from the banks of the Akropotamos—

or lay you out saltire in the sun, to be
picked at like Prometheus, down to bone.

May I call you *Alexander?* Will you bash
my helmet in, barefoot crush a scorpion?

The hour is getting late, and by now
you must want rest. I have paid

what some would call respects, two coins,
but forgot my tears in the village at home.

The backdrop of your life was always fire.
Persepolis is still burning in my mind.

Historic Spring

The gate wafts in the smell of rain,
its must and electric tang, the thoughts
of bracken telegraphing through the air.

The moss, a distant cousin, goes on soaking.
The just-add-water sachets return to life,
because they are simple. Because we are not.

The banked graveyards of Europe retain
wartime dead like bulbs in a raised garden bed,
while moss, grass, and clover compete for cover.

Too little water; too little sun. The pride and hope
of living things goes dormant for awhile, snoring
its spore-clouds upward, detonating in fruit.

Too much daylight; too much rainfall. Vines corkscrew
around a diplomat's neck, climb like approval ratings,
roots deploy their supply routes underground.

Green flags roll out their propaganda campaigns.
The insects are convinced. The airlifts begin.
Beetles rifle the leaf cover, ready for casualties.

America, Its Elements

I. Fire

Laughter makes the stars explode.
The smell of match heads and kerosene,
strawberries, blueberries and cream
salute *the Republic, for which it stands.*

The sky is blown apart with laughing stars,
bottle rockets and tracer bullets,
the black smoke of anti-aircraft flak,
tin toys and pinwheels spewing sparks.

Laugh, and the bombs laugh with you,
the stars laugh, too, the flyovers,
brass parades, gun smoke, and brimstone,
rockets' red glare and hissing fuse.

II. Water

A splash to prime the pump,
then get to know the sound
of water coming up
the pipework gasping
with each handle-pump.
In the throat of the well,
the bucket cries out.
The cloth dampens
on a bound man's face
while the body writhes,
silent crescendo.
Rain gurgles down the gutter.
Our lungs fill up with tears.

III. Air

The wind at night consoles me
with stories so frightening
I gather them into my sleep.

We raid the air for meaning,
circulate the breeze of opinion,
whip high winds of feeling.

Beside the stream, the reeds
are calling the name of the air,
the broken reeds, their open mouths

make a sound for this, *zeitgeist*, whistling
as it blows over goose-bumped skin.

IV. Earth

Only the tusks of this village remain.
The stars frown down on Babylon
with permanent rage, with penitent power
while the moon changes masks
at her pleasure. The starlight remains.

The azan complains in cinder notes,
a smoky haze in which to drown
the boat-like stretchers floating by,
wrapped in a sheet of sky, screeching
with the traffic of the unwashed dead –

remains of tissue, remnants of bone,
the stone walls of sunken wells, the water
black as blood, a bruise within the circle
of the town, its walls torn down by fire
and by water, and the fissure gushing red.

I give you my word, absurd, my hand,
both of them to have and hold, the bold
inscription on the turrets of my tomb: here
was a witness, pitiless, stone-cold, crumbled
dust, a man caught in a sandstorm, storming.

The Age of the Incredible

It flashes across our eyes, spiralling open the pupils,
which stutter over lines, pausing at the start of words
that progress – each more impossible than the last:

Human fingers are a delicacy in China. They incinerate
their own children to boil bath water in North Korea.
You won't believe what happens next. Go on, one click

to play the director's cut of a killer's YouTube rants.
Click to light on fire. Click to behead. Read commentary
on election results from certified netherworld trolls.

We longed for the day when anything would be possible.
The nerve endings open and close like spiked anemones,
tweeting like chicks in a tangled nest, hungry for more.

The grey sponge laps it up like spilled kerosene. We scroll
in our sleep, through hyperlinked dreams, Photoshopped
for effect. Remember. This is what we said we always wanted.

First Citizen of Bruges

(after the town legend)

The drone strike levelled the town,
and then the Vikings moved in, wearing
ballistic helmets and body armour, dogs
sniffing the ground for explosives ahead.

There was nobody left but me, and I hid
where I could watch, beneath the rubble.
Any wounded who moved they clubbed
to death, not wanting to waste bullets.

No slaves. No concubines. They silenced
every moan, scanning the corpses for warmth.
At the edge of the forest, a dark shape
paced on its fours, watching over them.

A raider lifted his crossbow, taking aim,
but his finger froze in the trigger, and from then
the bear was protected by rank, custom,
and it watched them into nightfall.

They piled the bodies and burned them,
stripping off jewellery and ammunition.
Sometimes a younger recruit would vomit,
spit, and then resume his undertaking.

They radioed in the good news to the oar ship:
beachhead established. They brought in supplies,
put up banners, and drank into unconsciousness.
I crawled into the forest. The bear kept watch.

Martyrs' Cross

Old St. Paul's Church, Edinburgh

Here is an icon to brand in the brain,
flat-hammered iron, irregular, dark—
A rail spike for the journey ahead,
foetus uncurled, shackles bent open.

Here is the flat blade that dubbed,
helmet's nosepiece, a horseshoe for luck.
With this you could bolt a door, wedge
out a draft, scrape a dust like dried blood.

Recall the arms now tied behind you
flung wide to gather up your child.
Some curl up, some splay, some dance.
And when you drop, this image ascends.

Here is a symbol to singe in the eyes,
spiking the track, hinging the door.

A Robot's Understanding of Friendship
for Vilfredo Pareto

One is special because they are specialised, able to
make the shell-beads you cannot. By swapping your
dried Caribou meat for strings of polished abalone
and conch, you add iridescence to your world view,
and the bead-maker gains tasty strength. Each tribe
profits from the trading, each goes away with *a bargain*
in his own language and so they meet, at equinox
and solstice, where the forest joins the black-sand
beach, pile driftwood into bonfires and celebrate,
join hands with their strange counterparts, hair and
clothes and piercings different, not-quite relations,
not-quite family, bringers of gifts, and barterers,
who come to be called *friends*, a category of fellow
man somewhere between the ones we try to kill, and
the ones we struggle to raise and protect from harm.
Even now, though the stakes have been reduced to
a single click on an underlined word, and instead
of goods, we now swap sensations, the economic
dynamics remain—I let you in, you let me in, just a
little more than Machiavelli would have advised, and
in this minuscule enlargement of two barely-existent
realms made of thought is a robot's understanding
of friendship, parading as words and images over
the sockets that once held our eyes, as we join what
used to be our hands across the flickering glow of a
fire so cold, it must be man-made.

Postcards from the War Hospital, Winter

I have run out of topics
for dreaming, so I make them up:
each morning, a new lie.

Under the dragon's tongue,
a tiny pebble of black saliva.
Each of us, our ignominies.

Always the war. We will
run out of morphine soon.
The radio flickers indifferently.

In my dream, I lose the leg,
and another sprouts in its place.
All night, I walk upon air.

Making Love to the Sound of Gunfire

after Ibrahim Nasrallah

let our muteness be

          like the pressing of hands together

cold at its core

          stones at dawn   night in their heart

embers going out

          let us make of our bodies a silence

clocks stop ticking

          the branches of trees hold their breath

our muteness is ours

          let the disc of the sky stop spinning

the starlight starve

          under the mask of our skin   the shush

of blood just pause

          Breathe into my mouth   me into yours

dip down into the well

          the clay jar splinters soundlessly

returns to soft clay

          let us shape it   and fire it   again

The Smoke

La Campagna, London, Friday Night

This is not your nan's Sunday dinner, a fish-and-chippy
or Chinese buffet. Tonight, this is Italy, no haggis
here, no bottled beers, just pasta, fresh, tailor-made.

The waiter gooses the posterior of the brawny
man in the scullery, then inverts his frown, glides
over to the long table of single women, and flirts.

At first, you think, he hears the clink of coins
on his silver tip plate. But their laughter opens
his face like a daffodil, peeling back the outer petals

to reveal the golden middle of a man surrounded by nieces
and sisters, their heartaches, children, and deadbeat men.
He recommends the right rosé to wash it all away

and they comply with his performance, casting their eyes
over his handsome face and fit physique, investors
in a scheme that yields only the thrill of investing.

But isn't this happiness? William Blake would whisper
in each ear an accolade for joy caught on the wing
and when they are at home, curling the stockings

from their legs, a little drunk, and over-full,
their smiles that say *could have been* and *you
never know* will smile on them again, shaking out

their hairpins, clink, on the makeup mirror,
a sound our Romeo won't know or hear, scrubbing
the stubborn Bolognese from his stiff apron,

sliding the tongue of the register back into place,
the backstage routine always tinged with sadness,
the afterglow of smiles, the space between applause.

Smoke Ring

Home Office, Croydon

Beneath the surface, darker matter stirs,
steaming up my third latte this hour,
gasping into the air-conditioned lounge
of what could be an airport terminal.
The man wearing a topi beside me
forgets to breathe, then gasps, repeats,
while his daughters in the play area
build homes from coloured bricks.
The clerks shuffle paperwork cheerfully
red passport, blue passport, green passport,
brown, jobsworth elves who know the list
of who gets Christmas, who gets coal.
My number up, I flash a tight-lipped smile,
Should I stay or should I go? stuck in my mind.

Clapham Junction

Should I stay or should I go? stuck in my mind,
the doors tweet shut with a rubbery thud.
*I'd beg for some forgiveness, but begging's
not my business* as the train glides away,
to float its fanning delta of branch lines.
Too little, too late, in the middle of a place
never meant to be anyone's final destination.
Here it all comes together, here it splits
wide apart. *One more change,* explains a dad
to son, tugging him across the platform.
Crowds weave together, and people disappear.
I step back from the edge, into the slipstream.
The train is gone, the moment past, but still
the ghosts remain, black shadows cast.

Soho

The ghosts remain, black shadows cast
on brick, mist over neon-lit cobblestones.
Hard Road is playing in the bar next door
There must be something in the air...
The exhaust pipe of a Hackney carriage
respires to the beat of its diesel drum.
In from the glowing tip, it lulls
then curls from a working girl's nostrils.
Visibly at ease, the smoke lounges
in all directions, spreading its arms.
Here is the city's grit-flecked embrace.
...been dying since the day I was born.
Part your lips, and breathe in slowly,
drawing up the sweet, unhealthy air.

Brick Lane Market

Drawing up the sweet, unhealthy air
from sizzling woks, flat bubbling crepes
we ogle falafel, smirk at t-shirt slogans,
finger the dyed silks and leather bags.
Huguenot chapel turned Russian synagogue,
now a Bangladeshi Mosque, the moon and star
wink down at our worldly commerce
from the smokestack of a silver minaret.
Every brick a different shape and shade,
pecked by the acrid air, specked with colour
from a rattling can, even graffiti is for sale—
Street art area: pay up or close your eyes.
Burning ghee and mustard oil, hissing paint.
Close both eyes, and follow the scent.

Canary Wharf

Close both eyes, and follow the scent
of marsh grass, salt rope, barnacled wood.
Oil lamps puff, pipe down their leaden light.
Tusk-like, whale ribs embrace a building site.
Spire of Narwhal, great barge up-ended, now
sea monsters rise up smooth, in cubic glass—
the streets scrubbed clean of tidal mud,
the Thames runs clear as lymph without its blood.
New brick, poured cement, tarmac's dull sheen,
cranes pick the horizon where gulls pocked the sand.
Shoe black, suit cleaners, flower shop for guilt,
security guards aim mops where coffee is spilt.
From a top-story balcony, an underwriter plans his grave
while admiring the skyline, its rich amber haze.

Blackheath

While admiring the skyline, its rich amber haze,
sun scalds the mist in an oil slick of light
reminding us the ocean is never far, reminding us,
like Turner, like Messiaen, in saturated tones.
Street lamps peer over us, considering our gait, where
the gibbet posts once dangled a peepshow of bodies,
betraying flesh to bake and rot its caramelised smell,
the gloaming air turned treacherous, picking rag from bone.
Beneath our dew-spotted feet, the earth grinds its teeth.
Sealed away like embers in the furnace of the heath,
plague pits chew ancestors' memories to tar,
the pocked bodies smelt, give off obsidian heat.
Over the vale, the mist descends, sherbet and blue.
Beneath the surface, darker matter stirs.

Two Women in Heels Walk Briskly Toward the Train Platform

It is twenty-seven against forty-one,
ball-peen hammers on a shingled roof.
Cuckoo clocks of the world, unite!
Fall out! says the sergeant at the bridge.
Seeds tumble down the rain stick,
match heads bounce on a hardwood floor.
They are marching through the gates,
they are hammering at the doors.
This is the sound of braille read aloud,
the ice in your teeth, 21 guns at will,
unwrapping the bubble-packed parcel.
Let us observe a moment of loudness,
give humanity a round of applause.

Calling all Stations Blues

Men on the platform in funny hats
shake their cans of change at me.
Chug-chug for the third world orphans.
Chug-chug for the veterans maimed.

The train does not favour the left rail
or right, but I touch the third rail
in asking, like a child, *Who caused the orphans?*
Was it the veterans? And who caused them?

Growing up, we would lay pennies on the track,
a form of worship, then collect the flattened
copper—more precious than money—a sign
that the inevitable had touched our lives.

Chug-chug calls the train to the widening night,
chug-chug its lullaby to the people inside.
The night is a keeper of secrets. The tracks
rise up ahead, dissolve behind.

Seraphim

You think of us in bright medieval paintings,
our flat profiles ascending and descending ladders.
And slender, robed in cinnabar, announcing from stage
right or praising God in cartoon bubbles flipped
upside-down to be read more easily from above.

But come with me to the bridge where couples
stroll over a brown-black Thames, haloed by domes
and spires, the spoked and spinning blue Eye.
Look closely down the railing. There she is.
We travel the chilled air, whispering: *don't do it.*

We are the shiver of thought, that the money or lover
might return, the painful illness be cured. And when
they jump, we are the warmth in hypothermia,
the ones in the brain's control room, turning the knobs
of the visible scene, hastening the fade to black.

Million-Dollar Rain
for E.K.

It is hardly there at all,
this feather-rain, suffusing
the air with casual descent,

pooling in crevices of husk
and trickling down the yellow stem,
dampening the topsoil sponge.

It is the antidote to drought, but also
to floods of Biblical scale, this
Providence and proof of tenderness—

each droplet a tiny silver dollar
skating the side of a piggy bank,
reclaiming the mortgaged barn.

How strange to discover it here,
leashing an eager retriever for his
pre-dawn hike through a London park,

four thousand miles and an ocean away
from where the saying first took root
in your keen farm-girl's mind.

Strange how what is hardly there
is there all the more for its gentleness,
dampening the head of your dog.

The neighbour dressed in misery still won't
return your smile, unaware he's breathing
money-mist, shaking gold-dust from his hair.

So you walk with this secret knowledge,
burning like a gas lamp inside, while all around
the land is soaking, gently soaking.

Tap Water

I think of you when I turn the tap, the alleged
seven others who have drunk this water before me,
or so the urban wisdom has run since Tudor times.

Some part of you is part of me now, sipping it.
The river is cold, but the body is warm, a fact
that makes us mammals wary, makes the kettle

an ally in the mist-damp globe of this floating island.
There was no moisture in my childhood, except in cactus.
An open river of sewage etched through sandstone.

Standing at the railing on Blackfriars Bridge, I lean
into the mud-scented wind like a ship's figurehead.
So much water. So many people. We thirst for our selves.

Geopositioning

I am the dot, the beaky-nosed dot,
travelling north-by-northwest. I am
the ghost dot drifting through buildings,
saint dot, blue halo pulsing. See me from
above. See me and be me, one right for east,
two lefts for south. You can't outrun your
own blue shadow. There is nowhere on Earth
you can go that I won't be you now. There is
only me-as-you, trapped in a tilt-board
labyrinth, steel ball rolling too slow and then
too fast past open manhole covers, around
squared corners, L-shaped wooden buildings.
This is not a game. These are our lives,
pinned to the back of the display case,
labelled by your postcode. I show you off,
saying, *Look at the me trapped in 3D.*
No one is impressed. Just keep walking.

Jellied Eels

We see ourselves through you, sweet
pickled blob, sea-smelling delicacy,
swimming into nets set east of Tower Bridge,
giving yourselves up for our supper.

Watery allotment, the sea-bound Thames,
scraped for cockles and dredged with nets,
your long fast swimmers mimic the current
dashing like Morse code along the wires.

Mish-mash of salty fish and tangy aspic,
green glazing for bombed-out cathedrals,
part meat, part skin, part isinglass,
looking-glass of flesh and quivering pane.

Alms for the clever, the slippery quick;
stretched ghost, half visible to the eye.

The Knowledge

Bright as a hurricane lantern, flammable as paper,
you roll a cigarette absently, leaning against your cab.
Something rotten wafts up sweet from a nearby grate.
You are fulcrum here now, the healer who healed himself,
crunching down alleys on a wobbly L-plated motorbike,
turning out memory's tricks, patting walls for coat hooks—
Lamb's Conduit and Buttery Mews, Occupation Road—
coercing new wrinkles into the brain, your chart, on each side
of a medial fissure called *The River*, which flows sin-black,
gorgeous, the crease in the book between Alpha and Omega,
A and Zed, horizon dividing sea from sky and light from dark.
You sleep with a Blue Book under your pillow, under a map
pinned to the ceiling, more accurate than planets or stars.
This is the contentment you were after, tapping ashes
through the slits into hell, your casual propriety simmering
a goulash of rat-runs and corner-cuts, faster by fifteen pence,
and this thought makes you look up to reveal a smile, the one
Eve first saw on Adam's face, wiping the juice from his chin.

Small Gestures

Forgive me, rose petals, my fingers
could not resist the habit of plucking.

Some would call it childish, and those
who waggle a shaming finger know best.

I do not own my hands, but slip into them
each morning like a pair of work gloves.

I flex to break up the stiffness, and they crackle
like damp embers stirring back to life.

They are all I have, these slender tongs,
to do what my mind instructs in the tactile world.

Sometimes when they mistype a word,
I wonder what they are trying to tell me.

Maybe they want to ask about the wartime practice
of soldiers shooting off their trigger fingers—

were they more afraid of dying? Or of killing
someone with a gesture as slight and easy

as curling an index finger into a teacup?
Oh, look what we have done to you now,

little flower. Let us sweep the petals quickly,
from one full-fingered hand to the other.

Meteorology

And then, it is over—
a break in the clouds,
which were never evil,
and the sun, which is not good,
streams into the wet yard,
glistening, not as a symbol,
but the simple refraction
of light. The rain and I
leave messages for each other
in this way, in the language
of facts: seven drops
on a mulberry leaf, a streak
of mud in the gutter, twigs
for divination, scattered
overlapping and apart. I give
the rain a few stacked stones,
offer up an old chair, one
I never liked much, let it
work away at the varnish.
And my mind, which is also
neither good nor evil,
I offer up now, to the sky's
window cleaner, the one
who summons the worms,
and scatters the trash,
that I might contain, someplace
in my own clay body, the gentle
indifference of rain.

Acknowledgments

With thanks first and foremost to Jane Commane for her many forms of dedicated support in bringing this book to light; to friends, colleagues, and mentors: Marvin Bell, Sandra Alcosser, Joseph Millar, Paul Stephenson, Chris Jackson, Isabel Galleymore, Michelle Bitting, the Highgate Poets; to my family on three continents; and remembering always John-Roger.

The following poems have been previously published in the following publications:

'Amuse-Bouche', 'I Was Born to Small Fish', and 'Two Women in Heels Walk Briskly Toward the Train Platform' first appeared in *Compose Journal*; 'The Argument' first appeared in *Magma Poetry*; 'Still Life with Bougainvillea' was commended in the 2013 Troubadour International Poetry Prize and appeared at coffeehousepoetry.org; 'Robin' and 'Seraphim' first appeared in *London Grip*; 'Ursula', 'The Hills' and 'Blessing the Bankers' first appeared at robertpeake.com; 'Making Love to the Sound of Gunfire' and 'Nocturne with Writers Block' first appeared in *Poetry Salzburg Review*; 'British Matches' and 'Soldier at the Tomb of Alexander' first appeared in *Aperçus Quarterly*; 'Martyr's Cross' first appeared in *The Galway Review*; 'Postcards from the War Hospital' first appeared in *Boston Poetry Magazine*; 'Have a Nice Day' first appeared in *Sugar Mule*; 'Sometimes I Wonder What I Do' first appeared in *The Long-Islander*; 'Despot's Progress' first appeared in *Orbis*; 'Unidentified Photo on the Internet' first appeared in *Martian Poetry*; 'Mr. Ergosum Speaks' first appeared in *San Pedro River Review*; 'La Campagna, London, Friday Night' first appeared in *Rattle*; 'Million-Dollar Rain' first appeared in *Harpur Palate*; 'The Knowledge', 'The Flies', 'Grass-Talkers', and 'Tap Water' first appeared in *The Space it Might Take* (Highgate Poets, 2014); 'Historic Spring' first appeared in *PoetryBay*. 'Jellied Eels' first appeared in *South Bank Poetry* magazine; 'White Pigeons' first appeared in *The Silence Teacher* (published by Poetry Salzburg, 2013, and this poem reproduced here with their kind permission); 'Last Gasp', 'Matins with Slippers and House Cat', 'Meteorology', and 'Small Gestures' first appeared in *Human Shade* (Lost Horse Press, 2011).